In memory of Alex.

BUSHEL
& PECK
BOOKS

Text copyright © 2021 by Bushel & Peck Books
Illustrations copyright © 2021 by Olga Zakharova

Published by Bushel & Peck Books
Fresno, California
www.bushelandpeckbooks.com

Bushel & Peck Books is dedicated to fighting illiteracy all over the
world. For every book we sell, we donate one to a child in need—book
for book. To nominate a school or organization to receive free books,
please visit www.bushelandpeckbooks.com.

A few visual elements licensed from Shutterstock.com.

LCCN: 2021931543
ISBN: 9781952239304

First Edition

Printed in China

10 9 8 7 6 5 4

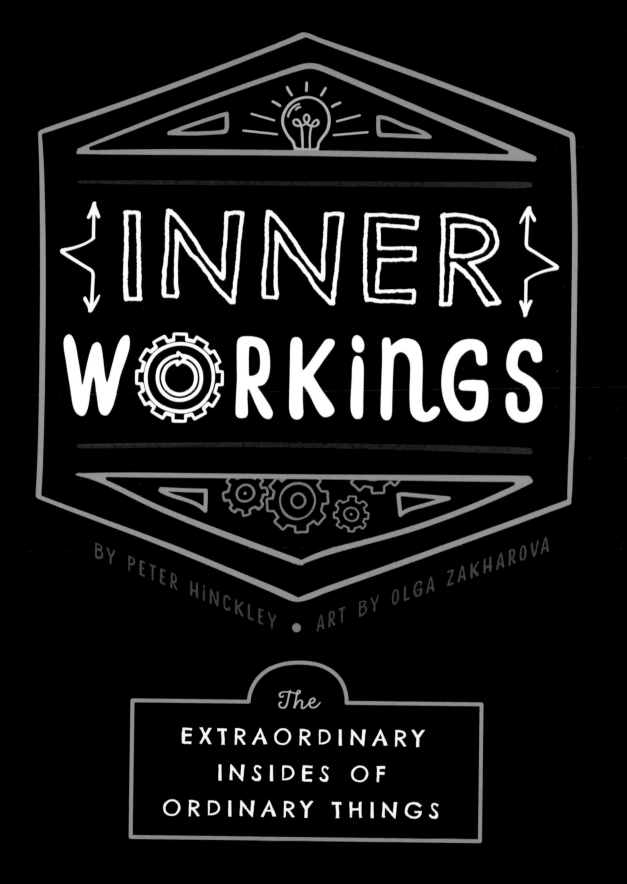

{INNER} WORKINGS

BY PETER HINCKLEY • ART BY OLGA ZAKHAROVA

The
EXTRAORDINARY
INSIDES OF
ORDINARY THINGS

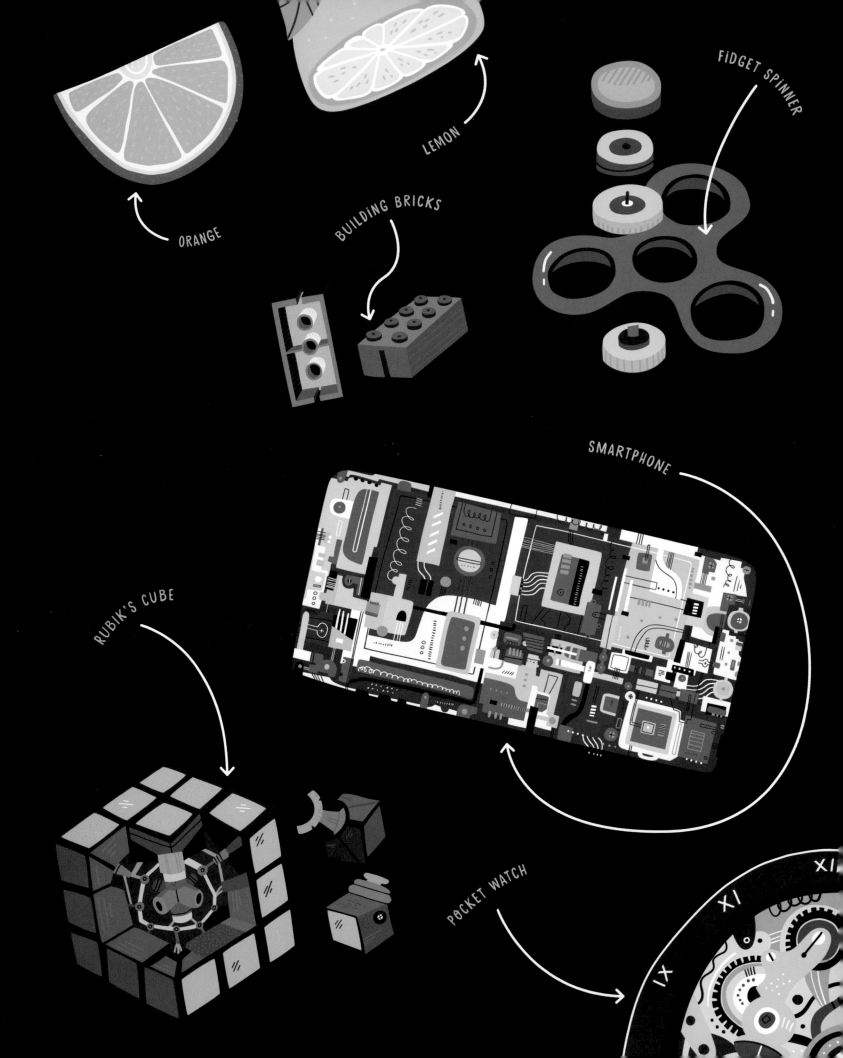

ORANGE

LEMON

FIDGET SPINNER

BUILDING BRICKS

SMARTPHONE

RUBIK'S CUBE

POCKET WATCH

XI
IX
XII

CONTENTS

XII

PINEAPPLE

APPLE

SMARTPHONE

STRAWBERRY

ROBOTIC VACUUM

P TRAP

"WHO LOOKS
OUTSIDE, DREAMS;
WHO LOOKS
INSIDE, AWAKES."

—Carl Jung

ALARM CLOCK

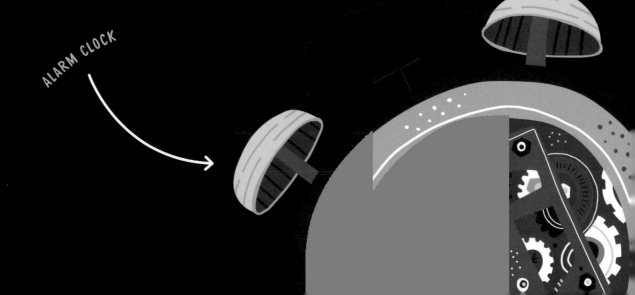

THE HORNET NEST

Hornet nests resemble a lumpy football and can be as large as two feet long. Unlike a beehive, which is constructed mostly from wax on the inside, a hornet nest is built from paper.

INNER COMB

The inside of a hornet nest is made from rows and rows of hexagon-shaped comb. But there's no honey here! The comb is filled only with the hornet queen's eggs. For food, hornets mostly eat nectar and sweet plants (like rotting fruit, *mmmmm*).

PAPER CONSTRUCTION

This isn't your mother's papier-mâché. By chewing on old wood and mushing it up with their saliva, hornets produce their own papery pulp from which they build their entire home.

"NIGHT VISION"

Did you know? Scientists think hornets are able to build their nest in pitch black using gravity as a guide.

SINGLE ENTRANCE

To protect from invaders, a hornet nest has only one way in and out.

OUTER COVERING

Thin layers of paper cover the entire exterior of the nest.

ROYAL BEGINNINGS

Hornet nests are started by a single fertilized female hornet, who becomes the queen. She builds the beginning of the nest all by herself! Once her first eggs hatch, the new hornets become the workers and take over the queen's extra duties.

THE BEEHIVE

construction! From the perfectly constructed honeycomb to the carefully sealed chambers, bees prove that they are some of nature's best engineers.

HONEY

Honey is made from flower nectar, which bees take turns chewing (bless them) until it turns into a sort of runny honey. They place the honey in the wax combs, fan it with their wings to cool it and help it thicken, and then seal the tops of the combs to keep the honey clean.

OUTER COVER

HONEY SUPER

Like the brood chamber below, honey bees fill wooden frames with wax comb. But instead of being a home for baby bees, the comb is filled with honey! When it's harvest time, beekeepers remove the honeycomb, making sure to leave enough for the bees to eat.

QUEEN EXCLUDER

This gateway is large enough to allow worker bees into the honey super above, but small enough to prevent the queen, who is much larger, from entering. This makes sure that the queen doesn't lay her eggs in the honey (because, you know, that would be gross).

BROOD CHAMBER

This is the main home of the bees. It's filled with wooden frames on which bees build comb-like structures from wax. Here, the queen bee lays her eggs. Those eggs develop into larvae, then into pupae, and finally into adults. The male bees become drones, and the female bees become worker bees.

HIVE BOTTOM

The opening is usually small, so as to prevent predators or robbers from getting inside.

THE MICROWAVE

Since it was first sold in 1946 as the "Radarange" (product names have come a long way), the microwave has become a kitchen staple. Microwave ovens heat food by subjecting it to microwave radiation. As the food absorbs the energy from the passing waves, molecules inside the food move around to try to align with the polarity of the waves (think of a magnet that flips around to connect with a piece of metal if the wrong end of the magnet is pointing to it). All the movement among the molecules generates heat, and the food is warmed!

COOLING FAN

Making microwave radiation is hot work, so the fan keeps the magnetron cool while it works.

MAGNETRON

The magnetron is the core of the oven. It generates microwaves by interacting electrons with strong magnetic fields.

WAVE GUIDE

The microwaves from the magnetron travel through the wave guide. The guide helps prevent the waves from spreading in other directions and potentially damaging other parts of the device.

MODE STIRRER

A mode stirrer spreads the microwaves around to help your food cook more evenly.

DOOR

Microwave doors are designed to keep the microwave energy inside the main chamber while still giving you a glimpse inside.

CONTROL PANEL

Popcorn? Reheat leftovers? The control panel helps you determine how powerful the microwave radiation will be and how long it should run.

TRANSFORMER

Microwave ovens need a lot of power, and the transformer helps convert the electricity from your home into a higher voltage for the magnetron to use.

CAPACITOR

The capacitor stores power and helps ensure a steady stream of electricity from your home outlet.

THE COFFEE MAKER

Coffee is made by running hot water over ground, roasted coffee beans. The oils from the beans mix with the water and produce—you guessed it—coffee. So just how does that coffee maker in the teacher's lounge work? It's actually pretty simple. And once you know the secret, you can royally impress your history teacher—but good luck on that lost homework. You're probably doomed.

CERAMIC HANDLE

MILK OR CREAMER

SHOWERHEAD

The heated water passes through what's called the showerhead, but no bathing here!

FILTER

Water drips over coffee grounds and goes through a filter into the waiting coffee pot. The filter keeps the ground beans from getting into the pot. And the coffee? That keeps sleep-deprived adults from a bad case of the crankies.

GROUNDS

DRIPPING COFFEE

THE COFFEE POT

WATER RESERVOIR

Everything begins at the water reservoir. That's the tank that holds clean water waiting to be turned into coffee.

HEATING ELEMENT

The water runs through a tube surrounded by wires that heat the water as it moves along. The heating element also conveniently keeps the coffee pot warm! May we shake the hand of whoever thought of that brilliant idea.

ON/OFF SWITCH

WATER TUBE

POWER CORD

THE BALL BIN

Balls have changed a lot since the early days of man. Gone are the sheep stomachs, the buckskins, and the webbed bird feet (yes, really). And of course, we don't sacrifice the losing team to Mesoamerican gods, either. No, today the design of sports balls is as much a science as it is an art. Weight, density, aerodynamics, and friction are all considered when crafting the perfect ball for a sport.

THE PILL

The pill has changed over the years to create bouncier balls that fly further. Of course, the commissioner of Major League Baseball has denied that, but it's tough to argue with science—so he doesn't.

BASEBALL

Baseballs have a core of rubber-coated cork (called the "pill") surrounded by layers and layers of ordinary yarn. A cowhide shell (sewn together with that classic red stitching) keeps everything compressed and wound tight inside. Recently, that stitching has been made more aerodynamic to reduce drag while the ball flies through the air. What Babe Ruth could do with one of *those* puppies we can only guess.

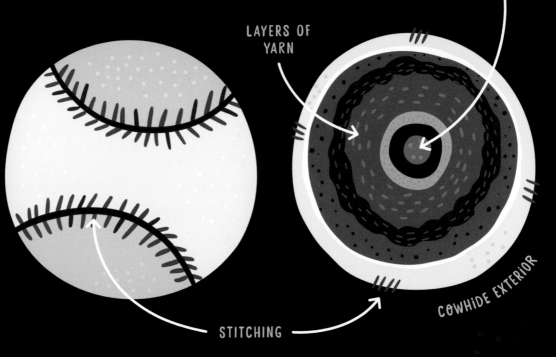

LAYERS OF YARN

STITCHING

COWHIDE EXTERIOR

RUBBER SHELL

PRESSURIZED AIR

TENNIS BALL

Unlike the baseball, tennis balls are filled with . . . nothing! But that *nothing* is super important to why tennis balls bounce. Inside the hollow interior is pressurized air. When the ball hits the ground, the rubber shell squeezes the air inward. The air then pushes back out at the shell, making the ball bounce up!

FIBROUS FELT

The fuzzy coating is usually yellow in color. Why yellow? Because broadcasters found it was easier to see on television!

CURVED SEAM

This is where the pieces of felt are sealed together.

HOW A TENNIS BALL BOUNCES

SPECIALLY
MADE
PLASTIC

BILLIARD BALL

Billiard balls are made from a type of plastic that is heated and squeezed to become super hard and resistant to cracks. Think those numbers on the outside are painted later? Think again! The colors, stripes, and numbers are all baked right into the balls themselves.

DIMPLES

The dots on the outside are called dimples. They prevent air from clinging to the ball, which helps if fly smoother (and further).

TEE

RUBBER
CORE

RESIN
SHELL

GOLF BALL

Golf balls are made from a resin shell and filled with layers of a rubber material surrounding a hard rubber core.

WEIGHT BLOCK

Varying shapes and positions of the weight block will make the bowling ball act differently.

FILLER
MATERIAL

COVERSTOCK

FINGER
HOLES

BOWLING BALL

The inside of a bowling ball usually contains a weight block surrounded by filler material. On the outside is a shell called the coverstock. This is made of different materials, depending on how one wants the ball to behave: plastic for beginners, resin or particle (little bumps) for advanced bowlers who want the ball to curve from friction.

THE BILLIARD TABLE

Though known to have existed as early as 1470 (thanks to dear King Louis XI of France), it's a mystery as to who actually created the first pool table.

GREEN AS GRASS

Did you know? Pool was based on earlier ball games that were played outdoors. The fuzzy fabric now on the top of most pool tables mimics the green grass of these ancestral games.

POCKETS

SUPPORT BEAMS

Supports hold up the green playing top and help keep it even.

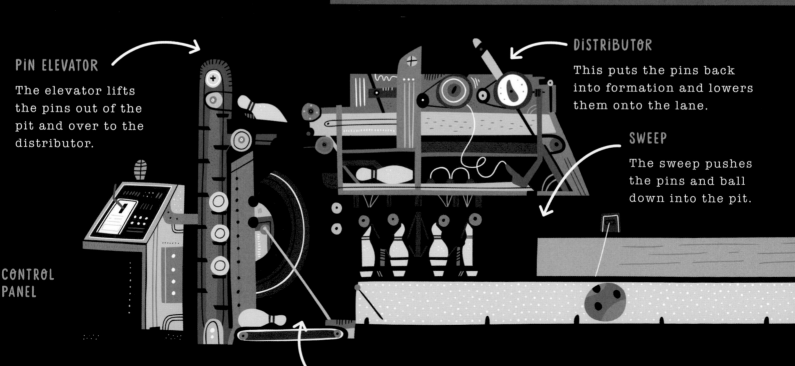

PIN ELEVATOR

The elevator lifts the pins out of the pit and over to the distributor.

CONTROL PANEL

DISTRIBUTOR

This puts the pins back into formation and lowers them onto the lane.

SWEEP

The sweep pushes the pins and ball down into the pit.

BALL PIT In the pit, the pins are separated from the ball.

To see the inside of a billiard ball, check out "The Ball Bin" on page 12.

BALL TRACK

Balls that successfully make it into a pocket roll down a track toward the ball dispenser.

SIDE RAIL

RENTAL MECHANISM

If used in an arcade, pool tables usually have a mechanism that requires payment to unlock the ball dispenser.

THE BOWLING ALLEY

The bowling alley as we know it today was first used in 1952. Before then, "pin boys" had to reset the pins by hand each round.

BALL RETRIEVAL

The returned balls are lifted onto a track and made ready to use again!

CONVEYOR BELT   The ball moves along a conveyor back to the players.

THE ANT COLONY

Like bees, ants work and live in large, cooperative groups called *colonies* (the fancy word for this kind of living is *eusocial*). Surprisingly, each ant usually chooses its own job—something like foraging, caring for the young, digging, or protection. Ants sometimes work with something called a *supermind*, where together they are able to make collective decisions as a colony.

iT'S CRAMPED IN HERE!

When a colony outgrows its nest, ants dig new passages and rooms. Some ant colonies have just a few hundred ants, but a supercolony can have millions!

OVER THE HILL

Ever see an anthill poking up out of the dirt? This is formed by ants tunneling underneath. The more they dig, the more dirt they deposit above ground, and the taller the hill becomes!

FOOD STORAGE

Some members of the colony take responsibility for collecting food. Each morsel they bring back to the colony is kept in a storage room, just like your pantry at home. But these aren't for the adult ants! Solid foods are usually only eaten by the larvae. Adults eat only liquids, which foraging ants regurgitate to the other ants when they return home. *Yum!*

EGGS

The queen lays eggs in a separate chamber.

LARVAE

The eggs develop into larvae. Larvae are blind and have no legs, so workers help feed them.

PUPAE

Larvae spin a hard cocoon and develop into pupae, who rest while they continue to metamorphose. When they emerge from their hard covering, they'll be fully developed ants!

ENTRANCE

Ant colonies usually have multiple ways in and out. This gives workers quick access to the tunnels inside. Can you find the other entrance?

THE TOASTER

The first electric toaster was invented in Scotland in 1893. Since it only toasted one side, you had to flip the bread and toast it twice. Fortunately, the automatic pop-up toaster came along in 1921, closely followed by pre-sliced bread in 1928. As for self-buttering bread, well, we're still waiting . . .

NICHROME WIRE

Nichrome, as its name suggests, is made from a mixture of nickel and chromium. When electricity passes through a coiled nichrome wire, it produces heat. You'll find nichrome in hair dryers, space heaters, and many other household appliances. In a toaster, this is what makes your bread warm and gives it all those delicious crispy bits!

LEVER

The lever pushes down a spring-loaded tray carrying the bread and turns the toaster on at the same time.

POWER SOURCE

TIMER

Toasters use different types of timers. Some are electronic, while others are mechanical (like a tiny egg timer).

ELECTROMAGNET

The electromagnet uses magnetic force to hold the tray down. When the timer is done, the magnet turns off and the tray pops up!

CASING

This covers all the internal components. But be careful; on some toasters, this gets really hot!

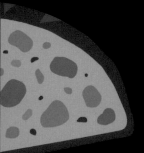

SOURDOUGH

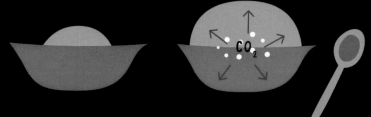

ABOUT THOSE HOLES

Most breads puff up before they bake because the baker has added yeast to the dough. Yeast is a living thing, and as it wakes up in warm temperatures, it starts to feed on the sugars it finds in the dough. As it eats, it gives off carbon dioxide—the same gas that makes soda bubbly—and this makes little air pockets that cause the bread dough rise. By changing the amount of yeast in a dough, the temperature it bakes at, how long it's allowed to sit and rise, and other factors, you can alter the texture of the finished bread.

TRADITIONAL WHEAT

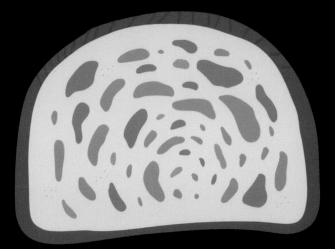

TRADITIONAL WHITE

BAGUETTE

CIABATTA

THE CAROUSEL

Don't be fooled by its charming exterior; the carousel was originally used as a military training tool for cavalry soldiers in the 1100s! In fact, the word *carousel* comes from the Italian word *carosella*, which means "little war." Only later was it transformed into entertainment for everyday folks, with the first carousel, as we think of it today, appearing in 1861.

ROOF

The roof protects the motor and machinery from the weather.

ALL THE KING'S HORSES

Given its military past, it's not surprising that the carousel still features horses today. But you'll also find tigers, dragons, elephants, and other exotic animals circling the center pole. Most are made from wood and painted in bright colors.

HOW DO THE HORSES GO UP AND DOWN?

Clever engineers found that by adding a bent rod underneath the horses, they could make them move up and down as the rod turned.

When the bent portion faces down, it pulls the horse down.

When the bent portion faces up, it pushes the horse up.

CRESTING

ELECTRICAL LIGHTS

DROP ROD

PLATFORM

CENTER POLE

The entire carousel spins around the center pole.

MOTOR

The first mechanized carousels were steam powered. Before that, they were turned by humans or animals. Today, most carousels use electric motors.

BRIGHT COLORS

The bright, primary colors on early carousels weren't just for fun. In earlier days, paint colors were less stable. By sticking with primary colors like reds, blues, and yellows, painters could more easily match the carousel's existing colors when doing touch-ups.

To see the inside of a paint tube, check out page 30.

THAT FAMOUS MUSIC

Today's carousels play music from electric speakers, but early carousels relied on built-in organs.

CLOCKWISE OR COUNTERCLOCKWISE?

In Britain, most carousels have animals facing to the left. But in much of the rest of the world, they face right!

CLOCKWISE

COUNTERCLOCKWISE

THE REFRIGERATOR

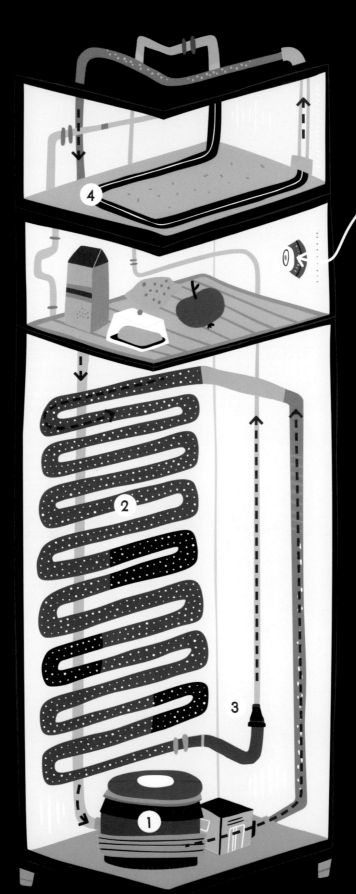

You might think that refrigerators keep food cold by pumping in lots of frigid air, but it's actually the opposite! Pipes carrying a material called *refrigerant* coil along the walls of the refrigerator. The refrigerant absorbs the heat from inside the refrigerator, and the result is colder air inside. Just how does that work? Take a look!

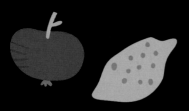

1

COMPRESSOR

The compressor squeezes the refrigerant gas and increases its pressure.

2

CONDENSER

The high-pressure gas travels through the condenser coils (these are the winding tubs you might see on the back of your refrigerator). The hot gas inside the tubes is cooled by the air temperature of the kitchen, and as a result, the refrigerant becomes a liquid.

TRY iT! Have you ever noticed that rubbing alcohol feels colder on your skin than water? That's because it evaporates faster. It's the same as refrigeration!

4

EVAPORATOR

As the gas expands, it travels through the evaporator's coils and draws out the heat from the inside of the refrigerator. This is what makes the air cold. The gas is sent back to the compressor, where it is put under high pressure again so the process can start all over!

3

CAPILLARY TUBE

The liquid refrigerant goes through a capillary tube, which allows it to suddenly expand into a gas.

THERMOSTAT

The thermostat allows you to control how cold the refrigerator gets. When it senses the refrigerator has reached a certain temperature, it turns the compressor on

THE DISHWASHER

Washing dishes has been a chore since, well, forever. In earlier times, dishes were cleaned with sand, ash, and even homemade detergent from a plant called *soapwort*. But no one found a way to get rid of the scrubbing until 1886, when Josephine Cochran invented the first dishwasher to clean dishes using high-pressure water!

LOAD IT UP!

Though early dishwashers required specific ways to load the dishes, designers eventually realized that people didn't follow instructions very well. Today's dishwashers are designed to get dishes clean in as many positions as possible.

SPRAY ARMS

The spray arms, often above and below the dishes, shoot high-pressure water from spinning nozzles to both clean and rinse the dishes.

FLOAT VALVE

The float valve detects when the bottom of the dishwasher has filled with water. When triggered, the float valve signals to shut off the water.

DISH RACKS

MOTOR

The motor powers the spray arms and other dishwasher functions.

CONTROL PANEL

Quick rinse? Steam dry? It's all controlled here!

HEATER

The heating element dries the dishes. It can also help keep the water hot.

ICE CREAM

Benjamin Franklin and George Washington were both known to have loved ice cream, and Dolley Madison became famous for serving it at government parties and dinners (her favorite flavor was supposedly oyster, by the way, and thank goodness *that* didn't catch on). But folks craved this sweet, frozen treat for many hundreds of years long before that. Early ice creams were often made with flavored snow, which Roman emperors were said to have sent slaves into nearby mountains to gather. Today, ice cream is usually made from a delicious blend of cream, sugar, and mix-ins, all frozen solid while being churned together.

Rocky Road

Mint Chocolate Chip

Strawberry

Birthday Cake

Cookies 'n' Cream

Berry Ripple

MIX-INS AND FLAVORINGS

Ice cream comes in flavors as wild as your imagination: from a shop in Philadelphia serving pizza ice cream, to a place in Missouri dishing up one made with cicadas (a grasshopper-looking insect)! But worldwide, the most popular flavor is still vanilla.

CHERRY ON TOP

Chester Platt is credited with inventing the ice cream sundae—with its signature cherry on top—in 1892.

THE CONE

The first ice cream cone was invented in 1896 by Italo Marchiony, who created an edible pastry dish for his ice cream stand. A few years later, a waffle maker at the 1904 St. Louis World's Fair introduced the waffle cone when the ice cream vendor next door ran out of dishes!

CONTAINER

SECRET INNARDS

Some ice creams are injected with cores of extra flavors, like cookie dough or brownie batter.

A TASTY MISTAKE

Fudge-making was very popular in the late 1800s, but fudge didn't always firm up like it was supposed to. When that happened, people poured the warm, liquid fudge over ice cream as a topping, and hot fudge was born!

THE SOFT-SERVE MACHINE

You know that ice cream cone with the perfect swirl? Turns out it's not *really* ice cream. Instead, soft-serve "ice cream" is made from a dairy-based liquid called the *base*, which is frozen while being injected with cold air.

EVAPORATOR AND CONDENSER

Soft-serve machines freeze the liquid base using the same basic technology as a freezer or refrigerator (see page 22). That means—you guessed it!—both an evaporator and a condenser.

HOPPER

The base is poured into the hopper, where metal beaters churn the base while it freezes. The result is smooth, semi-frozen soft serve!

HANDLES

NOZZLE

Controlled by the handles, the nozzle extrudes the soft serve in its characteristic pattern.

MOTOR

The motor turns the beaters and other machinery.

DRIP TRAY

FAN

The fan keeps all the machinery cool, which is especially important when dealing with frozen treats!

WHEELS

Try lugging this thing without 'em!

THE VENDING MACHINE

The first vending machine that accepted money was used to sell postcards in London in 1883. Since then, you can find vending machines all over the world selling everything from snacks to drinks, soup, pizza, smoothies, electronics, books, fresh bananas, and even live crabs! Because each product is different, each machine must be designed differently; the machine shown here is used for packaged snacks.

MOTORS

SNACK COILS

Packs of snacks sit inside coiled wires which, as they spin, advance the snacks forward.

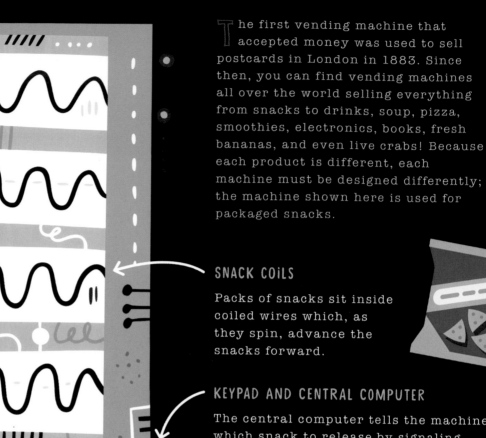

KEYPAD AND CENTRAL COMPUTER

The central computer tells the machine which snack to release by signaling which coils to turn.

DISCRIMINATOR

When paying with cash, the little port that feeds in paper bills is called the *discriminator*. As it does so, it scans each bill and runs it past a database to make sure the money is valid.

SNACK RETRIEVAL DOOR

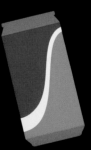

LASERS

A series of lasers (or other sensors) right above the door detects when a snack falls from a coil to the bin below. If the sensors aren't triggered, the machine turns the coils again until a snack *does* fall.

SIDE VIEW

THE GUMBALL MACHINE

Dispensing gumballs at just a penny each, the first gumball machines started appearing in the early 1900s. Today's machines are still fairly similar to their original counterparts, but don't expect to pay a penny anymore!

LID

To refill the globe, just open the lid. You do have the key, don't you?

DISPENSING DISC

The dispensing disc sits below the pile of gumballs in the globe. It has holes in the top, each just large enough to fit one candy. As it turns, gumballs fall out of the globe, one per hole. By adjusting the size of the holes, you can adjust for larger or smaller candies or allow more than one candy to fall at a time.

GLOBE

The globe holds all the machine's gumballs. These are always transparent, because how tempting would the machine be if you couldn't see the candy?

GEAR

COIN BIN

Deposited coins are collected in the coin bin.

KNOB

To turn the dispensing disc, you need to spin the knob on the outside of the machine. A series of gears connects the turning of the pieces together. One rotation of the knob will turn the dispensing disc just enough to allow one hole to be used.

CHUTE

Aside from being the most exciting part of the machine, the chute transports a gumball from the dispensing disc down to the retrieval door at the bottom.

COIN MECHANISM

If it's a paid machine, the coin mechanism will prevent the knob from being turned unless a coin has been inserted.

RETRIEVAL DOOR

PEDESTAL

HOCKEY TABLE

F irst created in 1969, air hockey was an instant success. Tournaments are now held worldwide with rules about the type of table, length of play, and even the color of the pucks!

AIR HOLES

Holes in the playing surface distribute the blowing air throughout the area of play. A well-made table should have even airflow across the entire surface.

AIR FAN

The heart of an air hockey table is its air fan, which provides the air pressure needed to float the puck along the playing surface. The level of pressure is key: too low, and the puck won't glide; too high, and the puck will ricochet out of control.

PUCK

The puck is a lightweight disc, usually made from super hard plastic (it takes a heavy beating, after all!). Though most games use a circle-shaped puck, pucks come in many other shapes.

RAIL

The rail keeps the puck from sliding off the tabletop during play. As in billiards, a clever air hockey player can use the rail for tricky shots against his or her opponent.

GOAL

On either side of the table is a slit-shaped goal. Sensors detect when a puck has entered the goal and send a signal to the scoreboard to tally a point.

STRIKER

Players each hold a striker to hit the puck across the table. The striker can also be called a mallet or a paddle.

PLAYING SURFACE

Though the pressurized air coming through the air holes is what gives the puck its lift, the material of the playing surface also plays a role. This is usually coated in something slick that reduces friction on the puck as it glides.

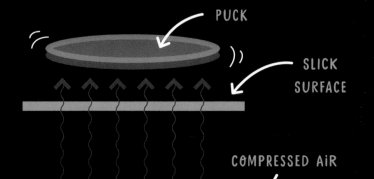

PUCK

SLICK SURFACE

COMPRESSED AIR

THE ART STUDIO

F rom cave drawings to the frescos of the Sistine Chapel, humans turn to art to laugh, cry, or enter worlds that only imagination can create. As with many creative endeavors, art is determined as much by the materials available as the hands working them. Whether watercolor or oil paint, colored pencil or charcoal, each *medium*, as they are called, requires its own set of skills and techniques to master.

PENCIL SHAVINGS

COLORED "LEAD"

PENCILS are made by encasing a stick of pigment in a wooden cylinder. Colored pencils use colored pigment, of course, while traditional pencils use graphite (though many people still call it lead, which it thankfully is not!).

WOOD CASING

GRAPHITE

PAINT

All paints contain pigment, which is made from tiny bits of colored material formed from chemical reactions, each of which produces a different color. To make paint, pigment is mixed with a material that makes it easy to spread and manipulate. What that material is generally determines what the paint is called, and there are three main types: watercolor, oil, and acrylic.

SCREW-ON CAP

To keep the paint from drying inside, the air-tight cap must be screwed on tight.

TUBE

ERASER

GLU ESTICK

Glue sticks are actually 40% water! But another 40% is acrylic polymer, which, when dry, causes things to stick fast.

PLASTIC CASING

WATERCOLOR paint is made mostly from concentrated pigment. When mixed with water by the artist, it creates a paint that can be brushed on paper.

OIL paint is made from a mix of pigments and an oil-based solution. Artists use this right out of the tube, though the paint can be thinned with a liquid called *turpentine*.

ACRYLIC paint is similar to oil, but instead it uses a base made from a chemical compound called *acrylic*. It can be cleaned up with water, but it dries much more quickly than oil paint.

TWIST-UP BASE

PAINT BRUSHES are made from clusters of bristles held in a handle. Brushes come in many shapes for different uses. A liner brush, for example, is extremely thin and can paint intricate lines. A fan brush, on the other hand, has a flat set of bristles shaped into a fan. What do you think this brush might be used for?

SPRAY VALVE

This releases the paint in an even spray pattern.

BRISTLES used to be made from real hair. Some brushes still are (some artists say those are the best), but many other brushes are made from synthetic hair.

PROPELLANT

This pushes down on the paint, forcing it up the tube.

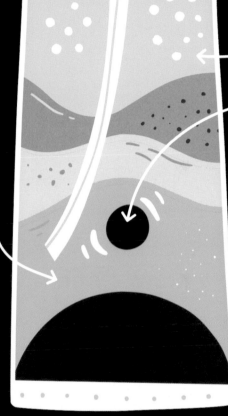

TUBE

PAINT

PEA

You know that rattling sound you hear when you shake the can? That's made by the pea: a small ball (usually metal, glass, or plastic) that helps mix up the paint.

SPRAY PAINT didn't start as colored paint at all! Its first use was back in the 1940s, when manufacturers used the technique to spray aluminum on radiators. Today, spray paint comes in countless colors.

HANDLES are usually made from wood.

DIFFERENT BRUSH STROKES

FIREWORKS

It wouldn't be the Fourth of July, Guy Fawkes Day, Chinese New Year, or almost any other holiday without fireworks! Fireworks have been around since the Song dynasty in China about 1,000 years ago, but the colored fireworks as we think of them today first arrived on the scene in the 1800s.

NOVELTY FIREWORKS

Novelty fireworks—like the ones you might light in your front yard—are among the simplest in design and the least powerful. A lit fuse leads to a series of compounds that create sparks, snaps, and bursts of light as they burn.

FUSE

This is the cord that, when lit, leads to the explosive material inside the paper wrapper.

PAPER WRAPPER

EXPLOSIVE MATERIAL

HOW DO THEY MAKE THOSE AMAZING COLORS?

By adding different metals or chemicals to the compounds, firework engineers can achieve different colors of light. Take a look at some of the most common ones:

red — STRONTIUM SALTS

orange — CALCIUM SALTS

yellow — SODIUM SALTS

green — BARIUM SALTS

blue — COPPER SALTS

purple — STRONTIUM + COPPER SALTS

white — BURNING METAL (like magnesium, aluminum, or titanium)

AERIAL FIREWORKS

Aerial fireworks are similar to novelty fireworks, but with two major differences: first, the fireworks are shot into the air from a mortar; and second, they are filled with gunpowder that explodes them apart in the sky.

STARS

Aerial fireworks have spheres of explosive compounds inside called *stars*. These burst into brilliant colors when ignited. As with novelty fireworks, different colors are created by adding various chemicals.

GUNPOWDER

The gunpowder bursts the firework apart when it reaches the air. This sends the stars out in all directions.

CHARGE

The charge helps delay when the firework actually explodes (because it needs to reach a certain height before it does!). It also helps ignite the stars surrounding it.

33

THE TYPEWRITER

The platen provides a solid surface behind the paper so that the type levers have something to hit against. To absorb the shock of the metal levers, platens are often covered in rubber.

Early typewriters became common in the late 1800s and lasted for a solid hundred years until the computer came along. Even then, many of the tools found on modern computers were copied from typewriters.

Typewriters work by hammering letter- or symbol-shaped metal levers against ribbons of ink, which in turn leave the impression of each letter or symbol on a piece of paper behind it.

PLATEN KNOB

By turning the platen knob, the platen turns and the paper moves up.

PAPER FINGER

The paper fingers keep the paper nice and snug against the platen.

TYPE LEVERS

Every letter or symbol requires its own type lever, which pushes against the ribbon when its key is pressed.

CARRIAGE

The upper portion of the typewriter is called the carriage. As a person types, the carriage automatically moves to the left so that each letter being typed appears one after the other.

TYPE GUIDE

Right in the center of the typewriter is the type guide, which is where every lever strikes when printing its letter.

RIBBON SPOOL

The ribbons provide the ink that type levers press against the paper. The most common ribbons used in the past were colored black, but red was another popular choice.

BACKSPACE KEY

Bah! Press the wrong key, and it's all over. Or is it? Backspace keys save the day with a variety of correction methods. Some typewriters mechanically scratched off the ink, while others applied white correction liquid.

KEYBOARD

Does the arrangement of letters look familiar? That's because it's the same way we type on computers and phones today! The keyboard is just one of many ways past technologies continue to impact us. But where did this arrangement come from? One story goes that a man named Christopher Sholes wanted to avoid typewriters jamming, so he designed a keyboard that put common letter combinations far apart from each other. Another story is that Morse code operators suggested putting certain letters near each other to make transcribing less confusing. Whatever the reason, by the early 1900s, thousands of typewriters featured the same keyboard arrangement—and it's been the same ever since.

THE VACUUM CLEANER

Carpet cleaners of some form have been around since the late 1800s, though a vacuum cleaner using suction didn't arrive until a few years later. Early suction vaccums had amazing names, like the Whirlwind, Puffing Billy, or our personal favorite, the Domestic Cyclone. Vaccums all work using the same basic principle: By pulling air out of the main body of the machine, the pressure inside decreases. Air from the outside of the machine rushes in to try to balance things out, and the result is a powerful suction force that cleans up dirt!

 FAN

A spinning fan pulls air out of the vaccum, creating the needed negative pressure.

1 MOTOR

An electric motor powers the fan and gets it spinning at top speed.

3

HOSE

Air from the outside flows in through the hose to balance the low pressure. Debris gets sucked up with it!

4

COLLECTION BIN

Debris collects in a bin (or bag), while the air gets pulled back out again through the fan at the top.

FILTER To make sure dust and tiny debris don't come back out through the fan, a filter blocks everything except the air from escaping.

LATCH

DEBRIS

WHEELS

THE CALCULATOR

PROCESSING CHIP

The key to a lightweight, compact calculator is its processing chip. Each time you press a button, the chip takes the information and works out the problem you're asking it to solve.

The first electronic calculators were invented in the 1950s and 1960s, and they usually weighed as much as two bowling balls combined. Portable "pocket" calculators showed up in the 1970s, with the first American version costing over $200 (which would be over $1,000 today!). Things have sure changed; a simple pocket calculator can now be purchased for just a few bucks.

DISPLAY

Data from the chip shows up on the display. Many calculators use what's called liquid crystal for their displays.

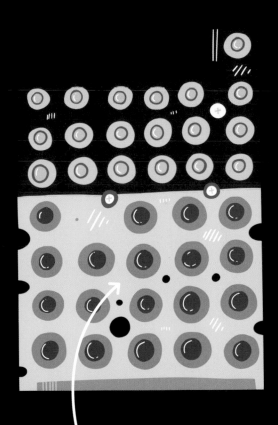

SENSORS

Sensors detect when a button is pressed and pass the information on to the processing chip.

BUTTONS

When a button is pressed, it activates its corresponding sensor beneath it. Buttons are often made from rubber but are sometimes plastic.

THE TOILET

It's well known that a man named Thomas Crapper (no relation to the infamous fecal matter, by the way) pioneered many parts of the toilet as we think of it today. But flushable toilets actually predate even him. A godson of Queen Elizabeth created a toilet that flushed with a water tank, and civilizations like the Romans used flowing water to clean their toilet systems even before him! As for toilet paper, well, that didn't come around until the mid-1800s—*ewww!*

TANK

The tank holds a premeasured amount of water—just enough to flush down what's, uh, left in the bowl.

FLOAT

The float is a rubber ball that floats on top of the water. When the water reaches a certain height, the stick on the float signals that it's time to stop refilling the tank.

HANDLE

When the handle is pulled, it lifts a lever that pulls up the chain connected to the flapper.

CHAIN

FLAPPER

The flapper is a rubber seal that stops the water in the tank from flooding into the bowl. When the flapper lifts, water rushes down and *voilà*! The toilet flushes.

BOWL

The bowl holds water and other, you know, stuff.

SOIL STACK

S-BEND

The S-bend is the curved pipe you see at the bottom of the toilet. It keeps some of the water behind in the bottom of the bowl, which helps block nasty-smelling gases from coming up the pipe.

WAX SEAL

THE TUB

The modern bathtub was first invented in 1883 by coating a cast-iron tub in enamel. This made a smooth, comfortable surface that was also easy to clean. Bathtubs today are, as a rule, usually five feet in length and are sometimes also made of fiberglass or steel.

COLD WATER SOURCE

FAUCET

The faucet is the magic of modern plumbing! By adjusting the knob, hot and cold water mix in different proportions to reach the perfect temperature.

TUB

Some tubs are freestanding, while others are built into an alcove in the wall.

HOT WATER SOURCE

DRAIN

The drain sends the wastewater down a separate pipe so it doesn't mix with the fresh water in other parts of the house.

WASTE OUTLET

P TRAP

The P trap works a lot like the S-bend in a toilet. The curved area traps some water, which creates a seal that prevents toxic fumes—or critters—from coming up the drain.

THE SHOWER

The first mechanical shower came along in 1767, the invention of a London stove maker. By the 1920s, showers had become commonplace throughout much of the United States, though it would take several more decades for them to overtake the bathtub in popularity.

SHOWERHEAD

Like an indoor waterfall, the showerhead releases a torrent of water from above. Adjusting the nozzle on the showerhead can produce different jets of water. Some showers even have multiple heads!

WET ROOMS

Did you know? In some parts of the world, showers aren't partitioned by either doors or curtains. Instead, showerheads are installed directly in the bathroom wall. A drain in the middle of the bathroom floor keeps water from pooling, and tile covering the walls and floors protects them from water damage.

HANDLE

As with a tub's faucet, the handle in a shower mixes hot and cold water. Cold water comes from the home's primary water source, while hot water comes from the water heater.

COLD WATER SOURCE

HOT WATER SOURCE

DRAIN

WASTE OUTLET

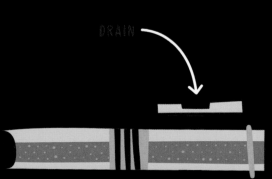

THE FIRE HYDRANT

pentagon-
shaped
bolt

VALVE

When opened, the valve releases the full stream of water from the underground main. The bolt on the valve is a pentagon, an unusual shape that makes it harder for anyone other than a firefighter to open it.

Invented by Philadelphia Water Works's chief engineer in 1801, the fire hydrant as we think of it today—a stubby, metal pipe sticking out of the ground—was actually just the next step in a long series of innovations to fight fires. Before then, many cities had pipes underground that could be accessed through a covering in the ground. And before that, when pipes were mostly wooden, firefighters actually drilled directly into the pipes when they needed quick water to put out a fire.

TO THE TRUCK!

Firefighters transport the water from the hydrant to their truck by hose. There, the water is pressurized and split up among more hoses to spray on the actual fire.

SEEING RED

Fire hydrants are purposefully painted bright colors like yellow or red to make them quicker for firefighters to find.

DRAIN

WATER MAIN

Fire hydrants tap directly into the local water main, which is the primary source of water running through a city.

FOOD

Ever think about how the jam gets inside a donut? Or why onions have all those pungent layers? It turns out that some foods are as ingenious as complex machines.

SHELL

The color of the egg depends on the breed of the bird.

CANDY CORE

INNER LAYERS

CORN DOG

Corn dogs are hot dogs encased in a layer of fluffy cornbread. To make them, hot dogs are put onto sticks, dipped into liquid cornbread batter, and then deep-fried until golden brown. They're a favorite at carnivals, and some creative cooks have even created other versions, like sausage wrapped in pancake.

JAWBREAKER

Jawbreakers have been around for at least a hundred years, though layered hard candies go back even further. They start with a candy center that is then covered in hundreds of layers of edible candy coating. Even with today's fast-paced factories, it takes several days to make a jawbreaker!

OUTER SHELL

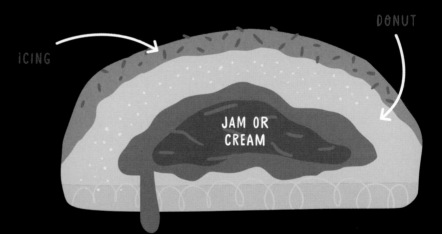

HOT DOG

ICING

DONUT

JAM OR CREAM

CORNBREAD

DONUT

Donuts can be filled with almost anything, though jam or cream are the usual favorites. The secret starts with the perfect dough, which puffs up into a light, fluffy donut when fried. The fluffier the donut, the more room there is for the filling, which a baker injects using a syringe—just like the donut is getting a shot!

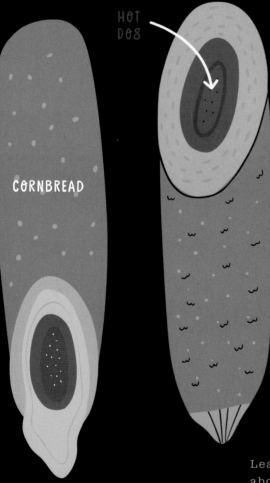

STICK

Learn more about what makes bread puff up on page 18.

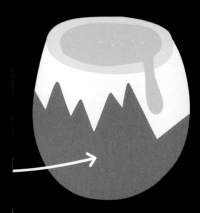

WHITE

YOLK

Most bird eggs have a rich yolk suspended in a transparent substance called the *white*, which is then encased in a hard shell. Chicken eggs are the most commonly eaten, though you can eat quail, duck, and even ostrich eggs.

ENDOSPERM is what forms most of the kernel and is its main source of fuel.

GERM is the term for the living part of the kernel. If properly planted, the germ can sprout and grow into a new plant.

CORN

The juicy kernels that surround a corn cob are the tiny fruits of the plant, arranged in rows. There will always be an even number of rows, with an average of sixteen on the usual cob.

ONION

Look at all those layers! These are actually thick, crunchy leaves that allow the plant to store fuel during the winter months.

TIP CAPS are where each kernel connects to the cob.

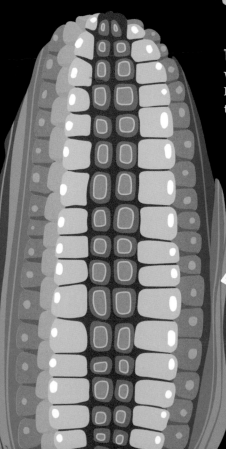

HUSK

CABBAGE

Round cabbages are the heads of the cabbage plant. Layers of tightly packed leaves give cabbage its unique crunch.

LOCKS

All mechanical locks operate by roughly the same principle: When perfectly aligned, metal pieces inside the lock allow it to open. When out of place, the metal pieces keep the lock securely closed. In a lock with a key, these metal pieces are usually a row of pins; in a combination lock, these metal guards are usually a series of wheels.

SHANK

The shank is the curved handle on the outside of a padlock.

PINS

KEY

When inserted into the correct lock, the shapes on the edge of the key position the pins into exactly the right places to allow the lock to open. Some lock-and-key systems have very intricate patterns, while others are very simple.

OUTER CASING

PADLOCKS

Padlocks are secured using hidden metal pins. The shank opens and closes so it can be secured around a latch called a *hasp*.

LOCKING MECHANISM

If the wrong key is entered, the pins in the locking mechanism will either prevent the key from going in all the way or from turning to unlock the bar.

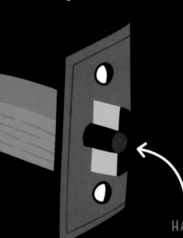

HASP

ALL LOCKED UP

As long as there have been crooks, there has been a need for locks. Mechanical locks have been found as far back as Roman times!

LOCKING BAR

This is the piece that actually holds the lock in place. It's made from a sturdy piece of metal.

PINS

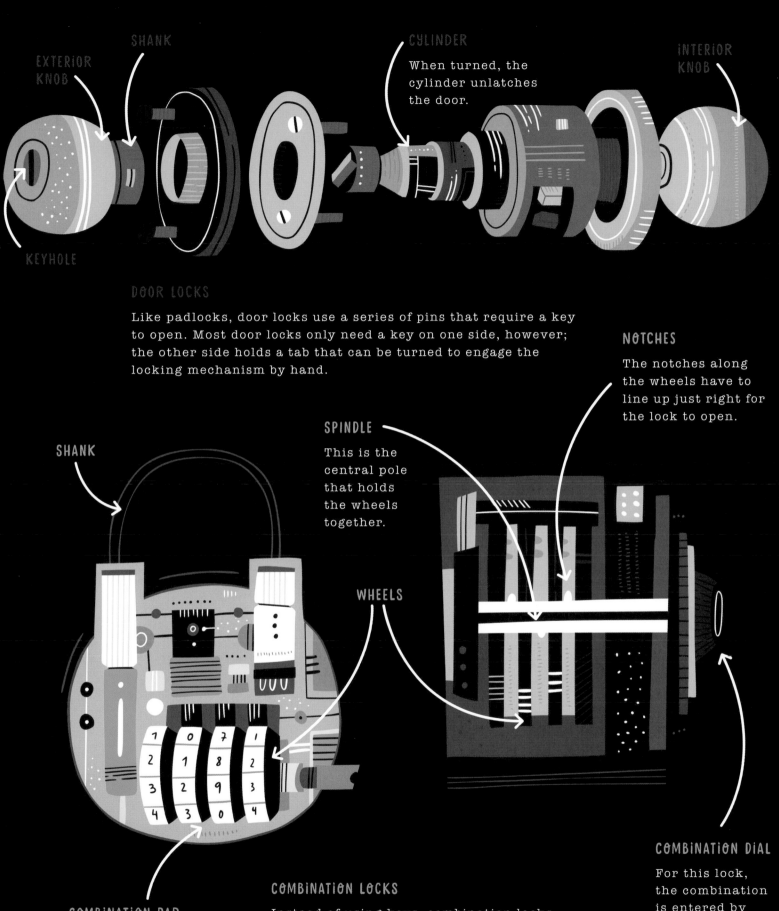

EXTERIOR KNOB

SHANK

CYLINDER
When turned, the cylinder unlatches the door.

INTERIOR KNOB

KEYHOLE

DOOR LOCKS

Like padlocks, door locks use a series of pins that require a key to open. Most door locks only need a key on one side, however; the other side holds a tab that can be turned to engage the locking mechanism by hand.

NOTCHES
The notches along the wheels have to line up just right for the lock to open.

SHANK

SPINDLE
This is the central pole that holds the wheels together.

WHEELS

COMBINATION DIAL
For this lock, the combination is entered by turning a single dial to a series of numbers in the right order.

COMBINATION PAD

In this lock, numbers are entered individually, each on its own wheel.

COMBINATION LOCKS

Instead of using keys, combination locks require a sequence of numbers or letters to be in correct order. These numbers are actually part of a series of spinning wheels that must all be perfectly aligned to release the lever holding the lock closed.

THE PRINTER

Computer printers recreate images (and text) by converting them into a series of teeny tiny dots of different colors, usually cyan, magenta, yellow, and black. When the printer prints those dots on a piece of paper using those colors of ink, it creates the image!

PRINTHEAD

The printhead moves back and forth across the paper and applies microscopic dots of ink that it takes from the cartridges.

STEPPER MOTOR

This is a special motor that can spin and stop very precisely. It moves the printhead back and forth so every dot gets printed.

COVER

The cover hides all the moving parts and keeps them clean.

DISPLAY

Through the display, you can send commands to the printer so it knows what to do.

PAPER FEED TRAY

The feed tray holds a reserve of paper for the printer to use.

ROLLER

The roller moves a blank piece of paper from the feed tray inside to be printed on. (When printers jam, this is often where you'll find the problem.)

INK LEVELS

These indicate how much ink is left in each of the cartridges.

INK CARTRIDGE

An ink cartridge holds one color of ink, though some have several compartments to handle more than one.

ABOUT THE AUTHOR

Peter Hinckley is the author of numerous books for children. He lives in California with his family and more books than he'll ever find time to read.

ABOUT THE ARTIST

Olga Zakharova (a.k.a., FaveteArt) is a self-taught illustrator and letterer with two bachelor's degrees that have nothing to do with art. Olga was born in Moscow, Russia, but moved to Latvia to find some peace and quiet. She now lives in an eco-village in the forest with her husband. Surrounded by nature on a daily basis, she finds inspiration in organic shapes and the perfect imperfections of the world. Her style is a mix of playful forms and cute characters drawn by hand and then digitized. When she is not working on illustrations, she can be found sleeping or being a doorwoman for her cats.

For a list of sources consulted and for further reading, please visit www.bushelandpeckbooks.com.

If you liked this book, please leave a review online at your favorite retailer. Honest reviews spread the word about Bushel & Peck—and help us make better books, too!

ABOUT BUSHEL & PECK BOOKS

Bushel & Peck Books is a children's publishing house with a special mission. Through our Book-for-Book Promise™, we donate one book to kids in need for every book we sell. Our beautiful books are given to kids through schools, libraries, local neighborhoods, shelters, nonprofits, and also to many selfless organizations who are working hard to make a difference. So thank you for purchasing this book! Because of you, another book will find itself in the hands of a child who needs it most.

WHY LITERACY MATTERS

We can't solve every problem in the world, but we believe children's books can help. Illiteracy is linked to many of the world's greatest challenges, including crime, school dropout rates, and drug use. Yet impressively, just the presence of books in a home can be a leg up for struggling kids. According to one study, "Children growing up in homes with many books get three years more schooling than children from bookless homes, independent of their parents' education, occupation, and class. This is as great an advantage as having university educated rather than unschooled parents, and twice the advantage of having a professional rather than an unskilled father."[1]

Unfortunately, many children in need find themselves without adequate access to age-appropriate books. One study found that low-income neighborhoods have, in some US cities, only one book for every three hundred kids (compared to thirteen books for every one child in middle-income neighborhoods).[2]

With our Book-for-Book Promise™, Bushel & Peck Books is putting quality children's books into the hands of as many kids as possible. We hope these books bring an increased interest in reading and learning, and with that, a greater chance for future success.

NOMINATE A SCHOOL OR ORGANIZATION TO RECEIVE FREE BOOKS

Do you know a school, library, or organization that could use some free books for their kids? We'd love to help! Please fill out the nomination form on our website and we'll do everything we can to make something happen.

www.bushelandpeckbooks.com/pages/nominate-a-school-or-organization

1   M.D.R. Evans, Jonathan Kelley, Joanna Sikora & Donald J. Treiman. Family scholarly culture and educational success: Books and schooling in 27 nations. *Research in Social Stratification and Mobility*. Volume 28, Issue 2, 2010. 171-197.

2   Neuman, S.B. & D. Celano (2006). The knowledge gap: Effects of leveling the playing field for low- and middle-income children. *Reading Research Quarterly*. 176-201.